Sense &

Holistic Approaches to Personal Development and Good Health

KL.Moore

A basic self help book to enhance your awareness, for those interested in Personal Growth, Colour and Energy Fields

Published by
Soul Traders Limited

ISBN 0-9540269-0-X

Typeset and printed by
J.W. Arrowsmith Ltd, Bristol

Dedication

This book is dedicated to my sister, Sylvia Cridge, who for many years worked as a nurse, bringing souls into this world and helping some leave it with great dignity. Her courage is still an inspiration to me and to those who knew her. She continued to serve her community even though she was having treatment for cancer, passing to the higher life 6 October 1996, aged 52.

Thank you for your love.

Acknowledgements

must be made to

All of my tutors in the spiritual and therapeutic fields.

To my students from whom I continue to learn.

To my friends who allowed me to babble on at great length and gave me their support and finally to Silke who gave up her time to give me encouragement and for allowing John the space to illustrate this little book.

John your kindness and enthusiastic contributions have breathed life into these pages and my gno-worm character – long may he survive.

I know that all of the people I am involved with feel that this information is worth sharing and that is important to help those struggling with their health.

THANK YOU ALL!!

Some of the proceeds to this little book will be offered in Sylvia's memory to assist those who face the same battle and seek to win.

Foreword

The intention behind this little book is to give basic exercises to increase awareness of energy and colour and to show the influence these have on our health.

It is hoped that this self help activity book will encourage you, the reader to explore and to have, as a result of that exploration, a better understanding of energy. Also included are practical ways to apply this knowledge in your own life; in fact to add tools to your personal tool kit!

It is a heart felt wish that this simple "How to" book will open minds towards new possibilities and assist those at the start of this magical journey . . .

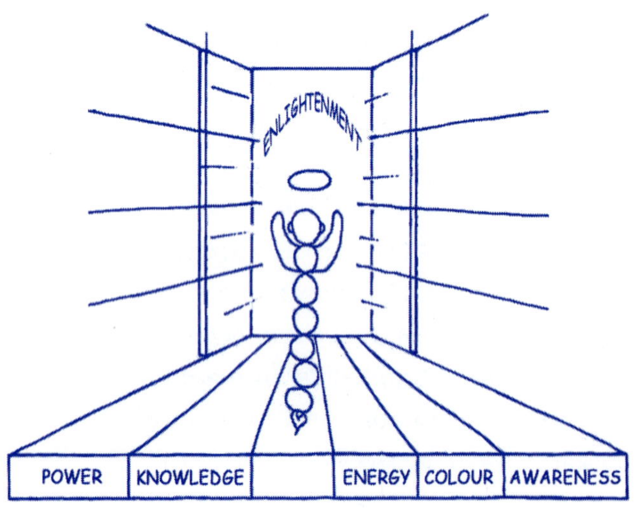
ENLIGHTENMENT
POWER
KNOWLEDGE
ENERGY
COLOUR
AWARENESS

Contents

Note *All Health Conditions should be checked by a medical Doctor*

The Gno-worm

Your tutor, helper and guide through
the exercises will be the gno-worm,
which is a combination of Gnostic
(having esoteric spiritual knowledge)
and the worm, who has the love of the earth

Section One

Energy Awareness

An Introduction to the Aura

- Anatomy and Physiology
- Chakras and Energy Systems

Your Energy Field and working with a friend: Exercises

- Seeing
- Sensing
- Dowsing
- Balancing

Balancing Energies: Exercises

Assessing	◆ Chakras	*Balancing*
		Using
		Meditation
	◆ Using Colour	*Self*
		Other
	◆ Using Stones	*Self*
		Other
	◆ Healing	*Self*
		One to One
		Group

Chakra energy chart

(See page 65)

Section One

Energy Awareness

An Introduction to the Aura

Anatomy and Physiology and Energy!

The human body is made up of cells. These generate a chemical energy from our food which is used by the body.

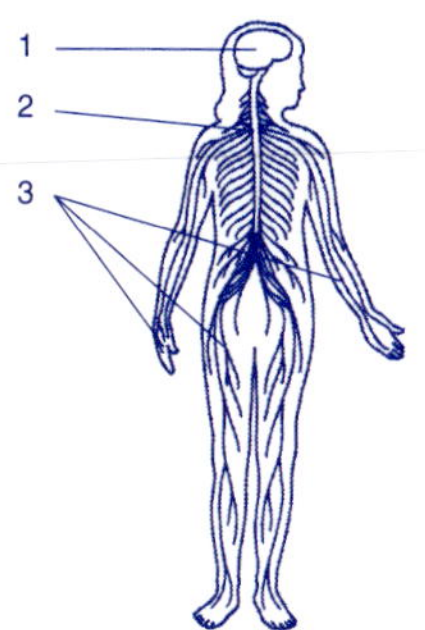

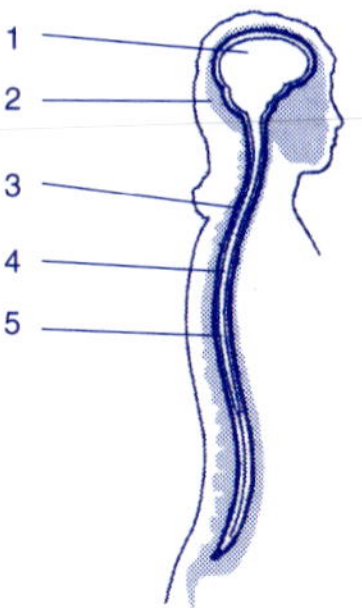

THE NERVOUS SYSTEM

1 Brain
2 Spinal Cord
3 Nerves

PROTECTION OF THE CNS

1 Brain
2 Skull and Vertebral column
3 Meninges
4 Spinal Cord
5 Cerebro-Spinal Fluid

The body is also motivated by a nervous system which has direct contact with a gland in the brain. This gland, the hypothalamus forms a bridge to activate the endocrine system which in turn produces a hormone to regulate the body's functions.

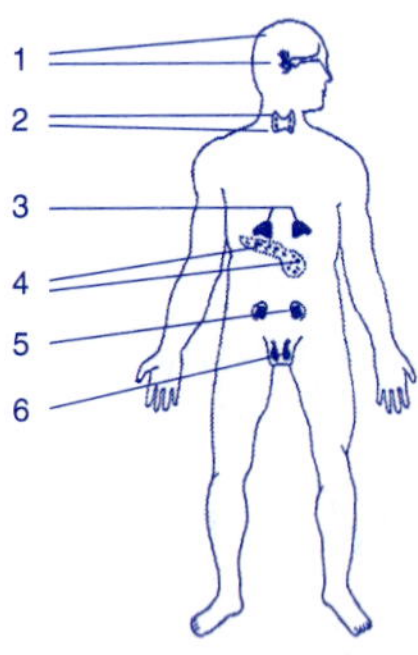

THE ENDOCRINE GLANDS

1 Pineal
Pituitary Gland

2 Thyroid Gland Parathyroid
Glands behind Thyroid

3 Adrenal Glands
(on top of Kidneys)

4 Islets of Langerhans
(in the pancreas)

5 Ovaries in Female

6 Testes in Male

All of the actions require energy and rely on chemical changes, involving particles which have electrical charges. So in very simple terms we are electro-magnetic beings.

Chakras and energy systems

All ancient medicines explain the human organism as an holistic being, that is, having mind, body and an energy field.

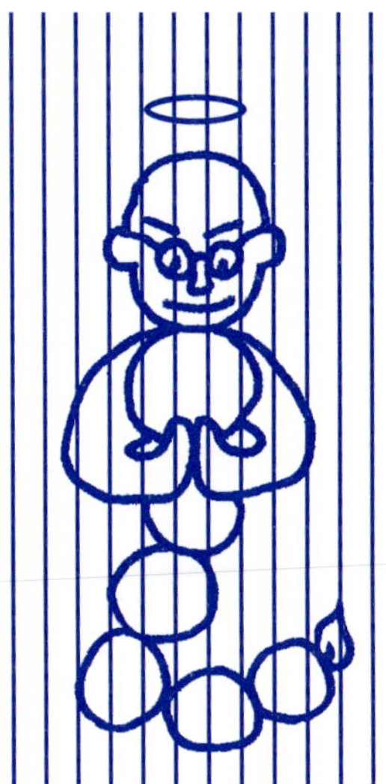

Spiritual belief systems are often included in medicinal philosophies e.g. Ayurveda, Chinese and Japanese medicines, also the classical medical schools such as those from the Egyptian or Greek civilisations.

Each traditional medicine, and there are many, relies on balancing the whole body, and so physical, mental, emotional and energetic systems need to harmonise. Examples of energy medicines in use today would be acupuncture, homeopathy or colour therapy.

Science has long since confirmed that the body has energy channels. These relate directly to the physical as the main energy centres are situated along the spine and in the skull. These centres are also closely linked to the endocrine (hormone) glands which affect our emotional and physical being.

And so it is that the energy systems permeate the body like a grid system of electricity and can bring good health unless blocked.
The main energy centres also have Sanskrit names and the word used for a centre would be Chakra, a "wheel" of energy.

Energy is absorbed into these centres from the earth and by our breath from the atmosphere.

The seven main Chakras follow the colours of the rainbow and at the base of the spine sits the red energy centre, and at the crown of the head sits the violet energy centre.

The energy system also radiates out from the body and can be photographed by Kirlean photography. The aura can be seen or even sensed (felt) by certain people. This ability can be improved by certain exercises.

The aura is generally perceived as an "egg shaped" energy field surrounding the physical body. The colours of the energy centres can be seen (Kirlian photography) to be a part of this swirling energy.

The auric field is said to have many layers: many ancient civilisations classify these as four "bodies" which are often given names eg etheric or astral etc.

Layers

- Physical
- Emotional
- Mental
- Spiritual

Your energy field changes depending on what you consume, think or feel, and whatever the surrounding influences may be social or environmental.

The nature of energy – Einstein stated that energy could not be destroyed and that it merely changed form.

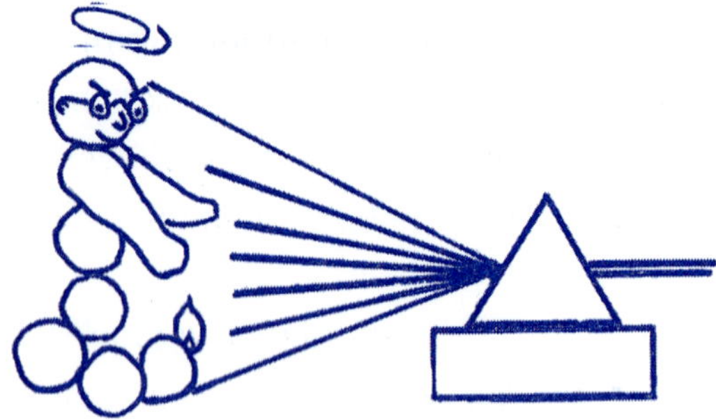

White light is in fact energy and can be refracted into the colours of the rainbow as shown in the chakra system.

All colours, sounds and crystals vibrate at a particular frequency and wavelength; so does matter i.e. our body.

Your energy field

The basic facts considered so far inform you about the nature of energy, it's relationship to vibrational medicine and some belief systems, and the connection to human anatomy.

Are you ready to explore this for yourself? Remember you can also do some of these exercises with friends or as part of a group.

It can be useful to learn to sense your own energy field. You may in time learn to see it. It can give information on your state of health and it can be "energised" or "debugged" and to some degree controlled by you. You can even have your own self help tool kit!

Energy Field Exercises – Seeing

ACTIVITY ONE

- Hold your hands apart and in front of you
- Stare beyond them in a gaze, you may see colour or a shadowing around each hand

Activity two

◆ Place hands closely together and then slowly draw them apart, you may see the energy between the hands

ACTIVITY THREE

- Try looking at the energy around a plant

ACTIVITY FOUR *(With Friends)*

- Look at the energy around the head and shoulder area of someone, you may see a cream/yellow outline
- Eye deceiving puzzles are usually good training for this!

Note The backdrop and light may make a difference

Exercises to work with Sensing

ACTIVITY ONE

- As in activity two in the last section, but now focus on feeling the energy field as it builds between your hands (it may feel like pressure or tingles or temperature changes)

Note The distance apart may need to vary.

ACTIVITY TWO *(With Friends)*

◆ Try to put your hands opposite their hands and feel the energy between your hands.

ACTIVITY THREE

◆ Try to push /pull their hands, energetically.

ACTIVITY FOUR

◆ Move your hands between theirs what can you feel?

ACTIVITY FIVE *(With Friends)*

- Stand in front of a friend and see if you can sense their aura with your hands. Place your hands either side of their head, move down to their arms, then their legs. How close is it to their physical body? Is it closer to the body on one side or does it vary from head to toe?

Activity six

- Now change position by 90 degrees and sense the back and front of your friends body by "sweeping" the energy field with your hands. How close is the energy field to the body?

ACTIVITY SEVEN

◆ Use your hands to feel the energy of each chakra. How does it feel to you. Are any of them registering differently to your hands? Are your hands being pulled in? If so, there may be a need to balance this on an energy level, before problems follow in the physical body.

ACTIVITY EIGHT

- Find the edge of the aura on a friend then have that friend expand their auric field. You should feel your hands pushed outwards from their starting point.

Note It helps if they can visualise the aura expanding as they breath.

Activity nine

- Create a "mental" brick wall at a point in your energy field. See if your friend can find where you have placed that wall. E.g one step or two or three steps away as you walk towards them.

Activity ten

- Sit in a room with your eyes closed and allow one of your friends to approach you. Just note how close they get before you sense them. Where is your sensing most acute? In front or behind?

Activity eleven *(for groups)*

- Sit in a circle holding hands; send energy to your right – stop, then to your left. Did you feel the movement of the energy? What other sensations did you feel?

Balancing Energies

Assessing the Energy Field

Increasing your understanding of energies, and learning to feel imbalances with your hands is just one way of assessing problems in the aura which may affect the physical body. An imbalance may often be something "different" or extraordinary that you feel as you "sweep" your hand through the energy field. E.g an individual may have an expanded energy field around one arm and the other one may have a very close energy field i.e. less power around that arm.

Dowsing can also be used to check the energy flow through a centre. For this you will need a dowsing pendulum, often some quartz crystal on a chain is used for this type of exercise.

Dowsing is and ancient art of divination.
E.g water divining.

Exercises: To Balance the Energy Field

ACTIVITY ONE: *Dowsing the Chakras*

- Check which way the pendulum swings for your polarity i.e. Yes/no, towards left in a circle or right in a circle. This may take a while, persist with it. To dowse the energy move the pendulum out towards your chakras. The chakra "whirls" should change direction at each centre. If there is not much movement, and the pendulum doesn't swing well for you, then that centre may need rebalancing. You can do this for yourself or for a friend.

ACTIVITY TWO: *Rebalancing*

- Breath through the crown of your head down the spine and out of the centre which needs attention. A few deep, slow breaths may be enough.

Note It also helps if you visualise the colour of the centre when you breath through and out of it.

ACTIVITY THREE: *Rebalancing*

- Use a coloured silk scarf for the centre that is out of balance; hold it for just a moment to absorb the colour that is relevant to that chakra.

ACTIVITY FOUR: *Rebalancing*

- Use the stone which is named for the chakra that is out of balance; hold this for a moment or place it in your pocket for a while.

ACTIVITY FIVE: *Rebalancing*

- Dowse for a gem stone which will have beneficial properties; it may be different to the colour you think you need! Yes and No swings of the pendulum will tell you this as you test the stones in front of you.

Healing

Rebalancing energies with healing is best done for another person, although you can ask for healing for yourself. It is also useful to participate in group healing as this “passive” energy benefits from the “battery” effect of groups.

It is thought that healing takes place on the etheric (soul) body and that the healer, as an instrument for universal energies, somehow transforms the energy field so that it can sustain and rebalance to varying degrees the physical form of the recipients. There has been much research into healing and it is known that there are changes in the composition of the blood of recipients and that some very positive results may follow.

NB There are organisations for teaching healers which have a professional code of conduct and an education system.

Exercises for Healing

ACTIVITY ONE: *Contact Healing*

A) Clear your energy system (Auric shower!) see chapter on meditation for this.
B) Attune to the universal forces of loving and positive energy by allowing yourself to be mentally passive and requesting help.
C) Rest hands on the shoulder of the recipient; after explaining what you are doing; advise them when you feel the connection is over .

NB It is important to have a positive attitude, make no claims and to leave diagnosis to the medical profession. Give thanks at the end of a session and monitor progress. Do not embarrass clients with inappropriate touch or in depth questions. You are simply offering yourself to a higher use of universal energies.

ACTIVITY TWO: *Magnetic Healing*

- Your energy field is used to supplement the energies of another, without attunement to the "universal energies" work with hands on the shoulders of the recipient.

NB This is an immediate boost but has a much more temporary effect than attunement contact healing and it can deplete your own energy levels.

ACTIVITY THREE: *Absent Healing*

- Sit and send out positive thoughts for the well being of the recipient. Asking for energy from the universal life force is enough.

NB Feedback is always useful

General Note: It is sometimes possible for healers and recipients to have energetic sensations during these activities; these do not usually last after the 10 – 15 minutes normally required for the healing session.

Activity four: *"Groups"*

- Sit as a group in a "horse shoe" shape holding hands, with the recipient at the broken space with a "hands on healer" working on them from behind hands on their shoulders. The group is usually a "battery for the energy" involved.

Activity five

- Sit a recipient in the centre of a circle of "healers" and send energy to that person.

Activity six

- Make a circle of "healers" and send energy around to the left, stop, then to the right. What do you feel? You should be holding hands, one hand palm up and one palm down as they link. Send the energy out to wherever you feel it is needed.

NB A candle or crystals may be placed in the centre of the group. If you close your eyes, do you see the colours? Can you feel the energy moving ?

Section Two

Colour Awareness

1. An Introduction to Colour

2. Interpreting the Colours

3. Exercises for Seeing and Sensing colour

4. Using Colour for Healing

Exercises

Self

Others

5. The Meaning of Colours Table

(See page 66)

Section Two

Colour Awareness

An Introduction to Colour

It has been understood by psychologists for many years now that colour can affect our moods. Much work has been done in this field by Max Luscher, and books are available on his work.
As a result of research some years ago, pink walls were used in the cells of "rowdies" at police stations; it calms them down.
A great effect!

Every day of our lives we are absorbing colour vibrations. The use of colour has long since been accepted as a therapy and more recently been combined with other treatments e.g. colour healing and crystal/colour reflexology. Theo Gimbel has done much to pioneer the use of colour as a treatment.

People use colour as a language tool e.g.
"I see red" and I am in a "blue mood"

As an important part of ones energy system the colours in the auric field reflect a persons state of health. Colour may be used to restore balance and harmony to the chakra system.

You can learn to see and sense colours. The activities for seeing colour are the same as for seeing the auric field. Colour swirls through the energy field, and usually there are three predominant colours.

Interpreting Colours

The next issue to face is that of the interpretation of colours. After several years of study I have designed the table given here in simple form which is a good starting point.

There are many ways of using and interpreting colour, and hopefully this chart will clear some of the confusion! This sheet does not cover shades, as this is a "basic level book".

Use your intuition for interpretation and, if in doubt, dowse for the correct colour usage.

Colours that you see may be clear or murky. If clear, all is well. If murky, a little balancing is required. Light or dark shades are seen by people at different levels of the auric field. You will need to be sure on what level you are perceiving i.e physical, emotional etc. You can then use the tables to interpret the colour and you may undertake to choose a method for balancing those colours; that is what is needed. The following activities give further details.

Exercises to Sense and See Colour

Sensing Exercises: With friends

ACTIVITY ONE

- Already covered in another activity – sensing with the hands; now try to sense colour from the solar plexus, extending your energy forward towards the other persons auric field. Imagine a TV screen and see the colours appear on it. Alternatively you may feel a colour or instinctively know the colours that are predominant. Try to find three colours and check the person to see if these colours are relevant to their state of health. (use the table; dowse to aid interpretation)

Activity two

- Using coloured paper or silk scarves, use your hands to feel the energy of the seven chakra colours. Use a blindfold and see how accurate you are at sensing the colours. At first they may just feel hot or cold; later you may become aware of the "feeling of green" for example.

Activity three

- Using coloured pencils, draw someone's aura and see if you can interpret their current state of health.

Activity four

- Have someone place coloured swatches near your shoulder. How do you react when sensing them?

Using Colour for Healing

ACTIVITY ONE

- Dowse your chakras to see if they are balanced – if not use the relevant colour in the healing ways to rebalance the appropriate chakra.

ACTIVITY TWO – *Rebalancing*

- Rebalancing with colour can restore your sense of well-being. Use coloured scarves to be held or placed in a pocket for a few moments.

Example – Red centre is out, instead of a scarf, wear the colour red and eat red foods.
Think red!

ACTIVITY THREE

- Focus on the chakra which needs balancing and breathe three times deeply through that centre and, at the same time, visualise the colour required.

Note If you re-dowse the centres after these activities you should see a difference in the energy movement of that centre.

ACTIVITY FOUR – *Hands on Healing*

- Using coloured scarves, place the colours needed over the client you are to give healing to. These may have been scarves that have been intuitively chosen or ones that you have chosen for them. Ask for healing as per the instructions in this book. Using these colours helps the client in a more immediate way, whilst the deeper healing takes place.

Section Three

Meditations for Awareness

An introduction to Meditation

- Candles
- Music
- Mantras
- Breath
- Visualisation
- Pictures

Exercises

Activity one	*Helpers on the journey*
Activity two	*Breathing for development*
Activity three	*Balancing with the breath*
Activity four	*Auric clearing*

SECTION THREE

Meditations for Awareness

An Introduction to Meditation

Often, meditation is described as "focused" relaxation. Many religions use this form as part of their belief system and would say that when you think you have "attained" a meditative state you still have further to go!

This quiet contemplative mindset is the basis of a considerable number of therapies and is known to relax the body and alter brainwave patterns to a slower pace.

In short, it calms the mind and allows the nervous system to relax, thus affecting all aspects of the physical body.

There are many forms of meditation, from a long, slow induction, such as one used to induce a hypnotic state, to the use of the breath as in pranayama yoga or, the use of a candle as a focal point. Mantras, words repeated in a chant, are also used, commonly in the Hindu faith and for transcendental meditation.

Music is often used as a tool to aid relaxation Visualisation e.g. focusing on a picture within the mind is another method to be used.

Meditation is an easy way to release tensions, as it can take place almost anywhere, once you are used to working with this method.

It is usually easier for the beginner to start with background music, or a guided (spoken) meditation tape. As the time you spend in meditation increases, external influences can be dispensed with and the silence may be all you need. Don't expect to be able to empty your mind and sit for an hour on your first attempt; Here are a few exercises to try.

ACTIVITY ONE

Helpers on the Journey (with friends)

- Use a relaxing piece of music, sit comfortably in the chair, perhaps you could work with a friend or a group. Ask someone to talk you through this journey and then you can return the favour, you may wish to put this on a tape.

Note Use this for connecting to those that work with you on your spiritual journey.
As you are seated, close your eyes and watch the breath as it come into your body and then leaves your body. Feel yourself slow and deepen

your breath. Imagine yourself stood in the middle of a green field, enjoying a warm summer's day. You can see at the edge of the field a path, you follow that path and this leads you to a gate. Open the gate and go through, continuing along the path, you are aware of the rustle of the trees nearby, the sounds of the birds and you hear the water flowing in a stream. As you walk towards the stream you realise that you are not alone, that a friendly and familiar person is walking alongside you. Arriving at a clearing you see a pool formed by the stream and you wait a while here. You can see the reflection of yourself and someone else. You stand and talk. After a while you then make your way back along the path near the stream and leave your friend at the gate. Closing the gate, to meet another day, you make your way back to the green field and then, gradually, you become aware of yourself on the seat in the room, feet on the ground, take a stretch and open your eyes.

ACTIVITY TWO

Breathing for developing your sensitivity and awareness

- Sit comfortably, eyes closed, with or without music. Visualise your auric field and your energy centres. Take a breath in through the top of your head and down the spine. Bring that breath out through the base (red) centre. To charge this centre up to increase your sensitivity, breath in and out of this centre just three times. Follow the above instructions for each of the seven centres, completing at the crown (violet).

Activity three

Balancing energies with the breath

- As for activity two but just breathe through the base centre to clear it and *NOT* in and out. Breathing three times at each centre.

ACTIVITY FOUR

Auric clearing

Sitting comfortably, eyes closed, with or without music. This exercise takes just a few moments

- Take a few deep, slow breaths, then visualise your auric friend expanding. At your feet there is a bubbly stream. As you stand a the edge of this stream the water bubbles up through your lower body, clearing each chakra as it passes through, up through to the head and out through the crown. The fountain of water sprays out through the crown and cleanses your auric field. You feel alive and refreshed. The fountain subsides and you again become aware of yourself on the chair in the room where you began a few moments ago.

Note This meditation is useful to energise yourself or to clear negativity.

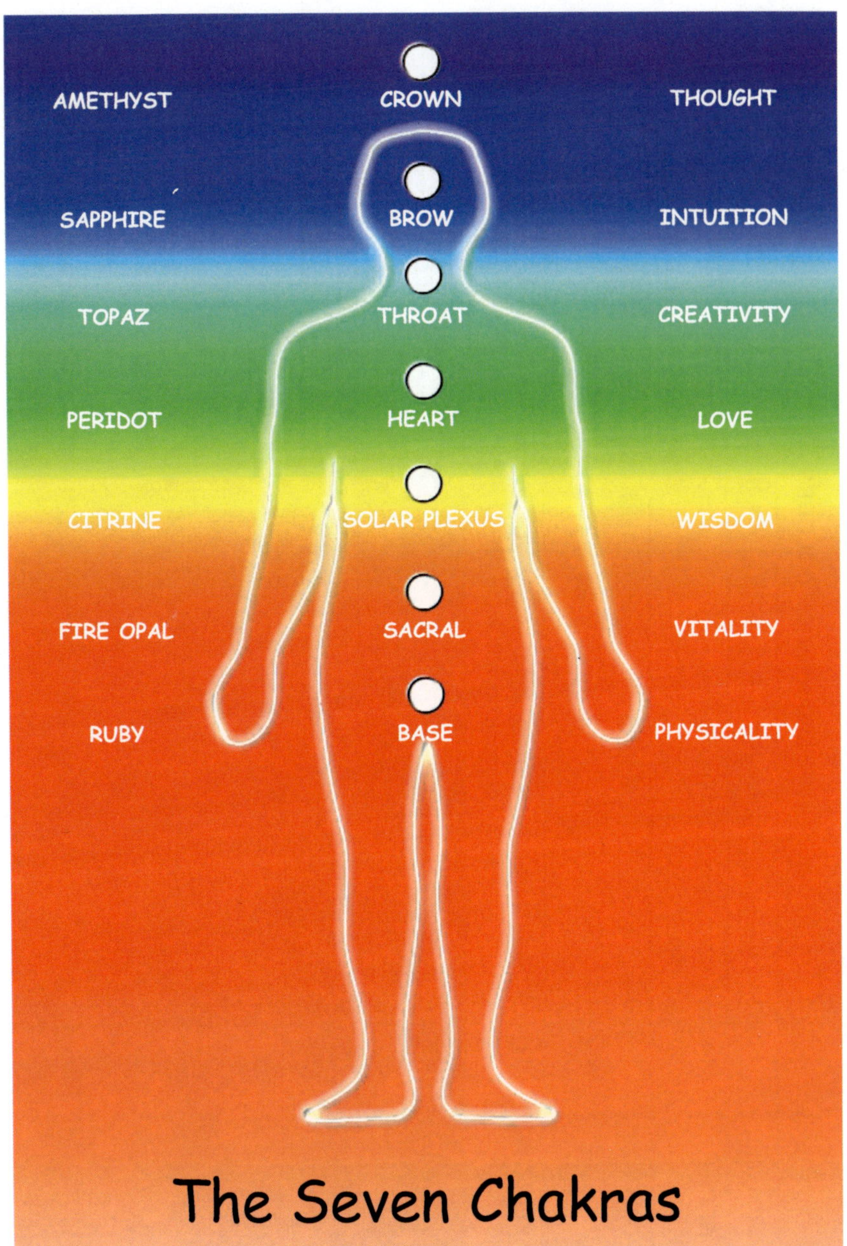
AMETHYST
CROWN
THOUGHT
SAPPHIRE
BROW
INTUITION
TOPAZ
THROAT
CREATIVITY
PERIDOT
HEART
LOVE
CITRINE
SOLAR PLEXUS
WISDOM
FIRE OPAL
SACRAL
VITALITY
RUBY
BASE
PHYSICALITY
The Seven Chakras

THE MEANING OF COLOURS

Colour	*Physical*	*Mental*	*Emotional*	*Spiritual*
RED	Reproductive, raw energy, sexual	Willpower	Anger, frustration violence	Physical mediumship, power
ORANGE	Digestion, bowel	Wisdom	Intuition, gut reaction	Psychic knowing, ener-gy used in various forms of mediumship
YELLOW	Liver, kidney, spleen	Intellect, logic, processing with mind	Joyful, positive	Knowledge, seeking, inspiration
GREEN	Heart, circulation, nerves	Balance, practical	Calm, stable	Earthly and spiritual balance, a good channel
BLUE	Thyroid, throat	Honesty and truth	Peace and love	Communication, teaching, philosophy, seership, mental mediumship, trance, healing
INDIGO	Pituitary	Introversion, isolation	Devotion, loyalty	Religious, potential not always fulfilled, dedicated
VIOLET	Headaches, pineal	Integrity, achievement, sympathetic	Spiritual love, humanitarianism	Higher spiritual mysticism and power

Section Four

Gem Stones for Health

An introduction to crystals and stones

- Balancing the Chakras
- Properties of some Stones: Table

Section Four

Gem Stones for Health

An Introduction to Gem Stones and Crystals

There are a variety of mineral deposits found in the earth. When mined, a whole range of crystals and stones emerge. Apart from industrial use, or for ornament, as in jewellery making, man has, over a period of time given value to precious stones and gems. Used in ancient ceremonies and religious rights, the Egyptians "powdered" gems and administered them for their health giving properties.

Stones and gems have electrical properties due to their mineral content and crystalline form. E.g Quartz watches! Certain stones have been categorised for their effects on health and moods. The energies of a room can also be changed by using these. In this "new" age, the ancient art of Fengshui has been rekindled to help energise homes and offices, positively. In this field, crystals are often used. They may negate the effect of the radiations from appliances in the home. E.g computers, televisions and microwaves.

Today, as with many therapeutic interventions, there has been a resurgence in the popularity of using crystals and stones for health. There are numerous books and charts to be found offering a chance for in depth study.

A table has been included with information on the therapeutic and spiritual values of just a few popular stones.

The properties of the “chakra balancing” stones are designed to facilitate a healing activity for yourself, with a friend or in a group.

Here are some exercises to experiment with, but you can also just hold the stones and see how each one affects you.

Exercises

ACTIVITY ONE

Balancing the Chakras

- Using the dowsing system described earlier in the book, check out the energy flow through your chakras. Is there one which may need balancing? If so hold the stone indicated in the chart and allow it's energy to blend with yours for a few moments. If you retest with the dowsing pendulum you will find the energy flow has improved.

PROPERTIES OF OTHER STONES

Stone	Chakra	Properties
Amethyst	Crown	Calms the mind and aids meditation. Strengthens the immune and the endocrine systems. A blood cleanser. Also has a good effect on right brain activity, pineal and pituitary glands in particular. Provides energy. Claimed to be a powerful aid to spiritual development, by bringing the lower nature of man to a higher level of consciousness. A friend to those who meditate also for healing, divine love, inspiration and intuition.
Sodalite	Brow	Enhances communication and insight. Strengthens the power of mind over body and dispels fear. As fear is removed, so comes calm and clearer thinking. Aids metabolism and the lymphatic system.
Blue Lace Agate	Throat	Calming; it eases depression, despair and releases inner beauty. Offers a sense of courage and fortitude, helps you to find truth and the acceptance of fate, while strengthening the body and mind. It contains earthing energy, it is also a powerful healing stone, can assist with circulatory problems, the colon, lymphatic system and the pancreas.

continued

Green Aventurine	Heart	Wonderful for initiating wisdom, understanding, humility and strengthening intuitive abilities.
Yellow Aventurine	Solar Plexus	Purifies the etheric, emotional and mental bodies. It enhances tranquillity and peace.
NB Both Green and Yellow Aventurine		Stimulates muscle tissue and strengthens the blood. Very much brain stones, aids in purifying mental, emotional and etheric bodies. Lessens fear and anxiety, by delving at the root cause. Balances the individual while also inspiring independence and well being.
Tigers eye	Sacral	Teaches patience, focus and concentration. It helps to develop the will to materialise our dreams. Aids the digestive system, also helps to ground the individual, giving better perception.
Haematite	Base	Brings about beneficial oxygenation of the blood, an energised spleen and will generally strengthen the body, helps with stress. Positively inspires will, courage and personal magnetism, while keeping the persons head out of the clouds. Helps us to separate our emotions from those of others. It helps us with grounding and with self esteem.

ACTIVITY TWO

◆ Dowse each stone for a yes/no to see which ones have the properties that you need to balance your energies. You can then hold these or put them in a pocket as you go about your daily business.

ACTIVITY THREE

◆ From the second gemstone table choose a stone and try it to enhance the "mood" of a particular room in your house. What are the most noticeable effects ?

PROPERTIES OF OTHER STONES

Stone	***Properties***
Carnelian	A highly evolved healer, helps with kidneys, pancreas, lungs, liver, gallbladder, aids tissue regeneration whilst cleansing the blood. Energising, balancing and connects the person to their inner-self, providing good concentration ability. Opens the heart to joy, sociability and warmth.
Diamond	Dispels negativity, purifies the body and spirit and reflects the desires of the higher self. Enhances brain functions, also removes imbalances in the personality. Amplifies energies in mind, body and spirit, inspiring innocence, purity, faithfulness, abundance and serenity.
Emerald	This "Unconditional Love" stone strengthens the heart, liver, kidneys immune system. A tonic for body and mind. Assists in deep spiritual insight, introduces the higher-self to the divinity within. Inspires love, prosperity, kindness, tranquillity, balance, patience and the power to heal.
Lapis lazuli	Strengthens the thyroid gland and skeletal system, it brings vitality and general relaxation to both body and mind. A powerful aid to psychic abilities and communication with the higher-self, inspiring great creative expression.

continued

Quartz Clear	This stone is good for brain activity, is also good for the soul. Eliminates negativity within one's own energy field and the environment. A good stone for meditation and healing.
Quartz Rose	The "Love Stone" encourages the heart to forgive and to exercise compassion by helping the person to let go of anger, resentment, envy, jealousy, through working on the spleen kidneys and circulatory system. Helps with sexual and emotional imbalance, may increase fertility.
Ruby	This beautiful red stone cares for the body and improves mental health. It represents affection passion and power. Promotes tranquillity, strengthens the immune system. A good tonic for mind, body and spirit. Links to the heart and promotes selfless service and spiritual devotion to others.
Turquoise	A healing stone, strengthens body, mind and spirit. Protects against environmental pollutants. Promotes creative expression, brings peace of mind, balances the emotional self.

Suggested Reading

Title	Author	ISBN Number
The Healers Handbook	Georgina Regan Debbie Shapiro	1-85230-022-1
The Unseen Self	Brian Snellgrove	0-85207-277-5
Healing with Colour	Theo Gimbel	1-85675-063-9
Your Healing Power	Jack Angelo	0-7499-1326-6
A Guide to the Under- standing and Practice of	Harry Edwards	(tel 048 641 2054)
Spiritual Healing Anatomy and Physiology	Kathleen J W Wilson / Ross	0-443-04243-8
In Health and Illness Spiritual Healing	Martin Daulby Caroline Mathison	1-85534-378-9
The Fine Arts of Relaxation,	Joel and Michelle	0-86171-040-1
Concentration and Meditation	Levey	
Meditation Workbook	Greer Allica	0-86012-193-3
The Holographic Universe	Michael Talbot	0-586-09171-8

Notes

Notes

Notes